Henry's Hat collection

A HENRY THE FISH ADVENTURE

Written by Megan Raugh
Illustrated by Elaine Smith

Henry's Hat Collection
A Henry the Fish Adventure

For Information: www.chaseyourimagination.com

This book is dedicated to my little fishes who
are making differences in the world.
And to all the little fishes who are also
making differences in the world . . .

Stand out!

Henry the Fish loved hats.
He had a large collection.

Henry was feeling stylish, so he decided
to wear a black top hat for the day.
Except Henry forgot that it was Sunday.
Time to leave for church, he thought.

When Henry got to church, Sally Squid
told him, "Why, Henry, you can't wear
that hat in church!"
"Oh? Why not?"
"It's not polite," said Sally in disapproval.
Henry apologized and took off his hat.

When Henry arrived back home, his friend,
Debbie Damselfish, called.
She excitedly told Henry,
"We're having a party! Come on over!"
Henry's eyes lit up and he accepted the invitation.
"Okay, let me grab my hat. I'll be there soon."

Henry showed up at Debbie's doorstep.
"Henry, you can't wear a chef's hat to the party!"
said Debbie.
"Why not?" Henry asked.
"Because we aren't in a kitchen!"

Feeling sad, Henry turned and went home.
"I just want to wear one of my hats today,"
Henry uttered to himself.

He rummaged through his chest
for the perfect hat.
"Aha! This baseball cap should do the trick! I can
wear it anywhere!"
Henry put on his hat and swam to a local restaurant
called Lettuce Eat.

"Excuse me, sir. You can't wear that hat in here," explained the waiter. "Why not?" asked Henry.

"Because this cove doesn't support that team."
"Oh, I'm sorry, sir. I'll take my food to go then."

Henry swam back home.
He pondered over what hat to wear next.

Options, options, options.

Henry put on his beach hat, and the
doorbell rang.
Henry answered the door.
"Hi, Mom. What are you doing here?"

"Hi, Henry! What's the beach hat for, sweetie?"
"I'm going to the Land of Fins," replied Henry.
"Oh, Henry, my boy. There's not enough
sunlight there for a beach hat."
"Okay. I guess I'll change then."

"What about this hat?" asked Henry.
"I can wear it during the day or the night.
Argh!
With an eye patch, I would have a complete outfit."
"Well, isn't this your lucky day?
I have one in my purse," chuckled Henry's mom.
"Thanks for the patch, but I still need a sword. Without
a sword to match, I'll have to try again."

"Will this do instead?"

Henry returned from another hat change.

"There's no snow in the ocean, silly. There's no need for such a warm winter hat."

Henry was frustrated. He mumbled and went back to dig through his chest full of hats.

Henry came back in a multi-colored propeller hat.
"What do you think?" He asked.
With care in her voice, Henry's mom says:
"I can see you are angry. Do you think that hat will
help?"

Flooded with emotion,
Henry screamed:

"I'M GOING TO
FLY AWAY!"

"Henry, honey, I understand you are upset.
Let's take a moment and breathe.
Remember hats are just things.
What really matters is
who you are on the inside. Don't let the
sea tell you who you must be.
Stand on truth without losing what is important
to yourself and you will stand out and make
a difference."

"Let's sort out your feelings and fix the problem, or you can fly away as you wish."

"Having some time to myself has helped me realized that flying away would be easy, but my mom is right. I will stand on truth without giving up what is important to me. I will make a difference. I can still be myself and have love for everyone else. Agree to disagree and still love one another."

"I'm proud of myself... hats included!"

GLOSSARY OF FISH

Juvenile
Parrotfish

Squid

Damselfish

Seahorse

Adult
Parrotfish